Bounce Me
Tickle Me
Hug Me

We thank
the Canadian Give the Gift of Literacy Foundation
and
the Leonard Wolinsky Foundation
for the funding that made publication of this book possible.

Bounce Me Tickle Me Hug Me

Lap Rhymes and Play Rhymes from Around the World

COLLECTED AND EDITED BY
Sandra Carpenter-Davis

ENGLISH ADAPTATIONS BY
Celia Barker Lottridge

PHOTOGRAPHS BY
Trevor Black
AND
Debbie Farquharson

The Parent-Child
Mother Goose Program
Toronto
1997

Copyright © 1997
The Vermont Square Parent-Child Mother Goose Program

The Parent-Child Mother Goose Program is a non-profit, charitable organization offering a supportive group program for parents and their babies and young children which focuses on the pleasure and power of using rhymes, songs and stories together.
All proceeds from this book go to support the program.

For further information
or to order copies of *Bounce Me*
write or phone

The Parent-Child Mother Goose Program
P.O. Box 68563
360A Bloor St. W.
Toronto, ON M5S 1X1
(416) 588-5234

The following organizations participated in the creation of this book. We thank them and all the adults, babies and children whose joy in rhyme has inspired us.

Creating Together Family Drop-In Centre
Jessie's Centre For Teenagers
More Than Child's Play
Parkdale Community Health Centre
South Asian Women's Centre
Baby's Best Start for Brighter Futures programs at:
Gordon Ridge Community Centre
West Hill Community Services Adult/Child Centre
All the teachers and participants in the Parent-Child Mother Goose Programs

Photo on page 19 by Debbie Farquharson. All other photos by Trevor Black.

Canadian Cataloguing in Publication Data

Main entry under title:

Bounce me, tickle me, hug me: lap rhymes and play rhymes from around the world

Rhymes in original language with English adaptations.
ISBN 0-9681462-2-8

1. Nursery rhymes. 2. Children's poetry. I. Lottridge, Celia B. (Celia Barker).
II. Carpenter-Davis, Sandra, 1945– . III. Parent-Child Mother Goose Program.

PZ8.3.B68 1997   398.8   C97-932189-1

DESIGN AND PRODUCTION BY MOVEABLE TYPE INC., TORONTO. PRINTED IN CANADA BY WOOD PRINTING AND GRAPHICS INC.
DISTRIBUTED TO THE BOOK TRADE IN CANADA BY GROUNDWOOD BOOKS.

How This Book Came to Be

You are not likely to find anything quite like this little book. Let me tell you how it came to be.

An important purpose of the Parent-Child Mother Goose Program is to share rhymes, songs and stories with mothers, fathers and other caregivers and their babies. Over the years, our groups have included people from many parts of the world and we have found ourselves learning wonderful rhymes which the participants have shared with us.

We soon realized that we have a rich, multicultural garden from which to gather new material to use in our program. But our program reaches only a few hundred parents and children each year. We knew that, in our wider community, there were more rhymes to be collected and more people who would enjoy them. A book was the answer. And so *Bounce Me, Tickle Me, Hug Me* was born.

Collecting the rhymes turned out to be both a pleasure and a challenge. We wished to represent as many cultures and languages as possible, but our resources were limited. So, we started with the people we knew. More than half of the rhymes in this book were collected from participants and teachers in our programs. Others have come from parents, grandparents, teachers and others who heard of our quest. Some contributors were recent immigrants, while others who were born here had family still fluently speaking their language of origin.

The process of collecting these rhymes was interesting and seldom easy. Quite often when someone was first asked if they remembered a childhood rhyme, they believed they had no rhymes to share. But that was seldom the end of it. When approached again, many people began to remember bits and pieces of rhyme and song. Parents contacted grandparents, aunts and uncles. Often the missing words (and more) were found; always old memories were rediscovered. People were sometimes surprised that anyone would be interested in such childish things as baby rhymes or the experiences of so long ago in another culture. With persistent encouragement many people felt comfortable enough to travel back to their childhoods not only for rhymes to share with us, but for stories for their families. We believe the project helped to foster understanding of just how valuable to families such memories are. I know the sharing continues.

Sometimes, the process worked almost magically. At a drop-in centre one day, I first shared a Jamaican rhyme I knew. Then several women told me versions of the same rhyme from all over the Caribbean! It didn't stop there: we exchanged rhymes and songs and had a wonderful conversation about childhood experiences.

We ended up with a wealth of rhymes. For the purpose of this book we selected those that were especially suited to being used interactively with babies and toddlers and that could be translated effectively into English. We also wanted to convey the way the rhymes are used by the people we collected them from. The directions and notes included with each rhyme reflect this information.

These rhymes are meant for you to enjoy with a child! There is no right or wrong way to use them. They have now been passed down to you and it's your turn to adapt them. Add your child's name. Make changes in actions or words, or set the words to music. Make the rhymes your own.

We hope this book will be used by families and by people working in intercultural settings with children and parents. We also hope that it will encourage everyone to keep songs, rhymes and stories from their cultures alive – not just for the children, but for the parents and elders as well.

Sandra Carpenter-Davis
Storyteller/Teacher
The Parent-Child Mother Goose Program

Table of Contents

Foreword	viii	
Bulgarian	1	Bouncy, Bouncy, Horsey
Caribbean (Jamaica)	2	Mosquito One, Mosquito Two
	3	Mama Buy Bread
Caribbean (St. Vincent)	4	Poor Henreetta
Chinese	5	One Little Bug
	6	Little Monkey in a Tree
French	7	Little Chicken on the Wall
German	8	This One's the Thumb
Greek	9	Here Goes the Rabbit
Hindi	10	Sleep, Small Baby, Sleep
Hungarian	11	Caw, Caw, Jackdaw
	12	Thitch-thatch
Irish	13	Poor Wee Me
	13	This Is the Way Me Father Taught Me
Italian	14	Clap, Clap, Clap Your Hands
Japanese	15	Two, Two, What Are Two?
Portuguese	16	Peck, Peck, Peck…
	17	Here's the Hen
Punjabi	18	Ride the Horsey
Serbian	19	Clap, Clap, Clap Your Hands
Spanish	20	This Little Pig
Tamil	21	Moon, Moon, Come to Us, Moon
	22	We're Hungry!
Ukrainian	24	Peas, Potatoes, Beans
	25	Ahh, Ahh, Two Little Cats
Urdu	26	Sleep, My Darling Moon
Vietnamese	27	Look, There's a White Horse!
Yiddish	28	Earkin-Hearkin
	29	Bazoo, Bazoo
Inuktitut (Eastern Arctic)	30	A Lullaby
Appendices	32	A Note on the Text
	34	Literal Translations

Foreword

This collection is an extraordinary one, as exceptional among Canadian books about young children and parenting as the Parent-Child Mother Goose Program is among cultural activities in Canada. Many of this country's wealth of cultural groups are represented here, but this is not another multicultural collection that merely samples diversity. Rather, it offers a rare intercultural opportunity to access and more fully appreciate a multiplicity of tradition through commonalities of needs and experience. For this book is about communication – between adults and the very young, among adults who are or were parents as well as, it is hoped, among all Canadians of the future.

People around the world and through time have had need for easy ways to interact meaningfully with their young, to communicate their affection, interests and concerns to wee ones who have acquired few verbal means to reciprocate. Therefore, these rhymes, songs and games tend to involve action – an adult rocking a baby if not bouncing the child or indicating her hands, toes and such. They usually have regular rhyming, lots of repetition and simple melodies – to accommodate the shyest of adult voices and weakest of memories as much as to teach children basic language patterns, rhythm and harmony. And they deal with common things in nature or about being human.

These little and seemingly insignificant rhymes are, then, supremely humane, representing some of the most significant experiences of our lives – the adult-child, and especially parent-child, connections of our earliest times. And the rhymes remain with us, stored away for years and popping into memory (often only as fragments or profound remembrances) in circumstances appropriate for their use – when older people seek to communicate with the very young who themselves have great need of the rhymes and the experiences involving them.

The Parent-Child Mother Goose Program enables these experiences, providing situations that encourage adults to recover, value and share their own memories with each other and, most importantly, with their children. The significance of this program will resonate through generations to come.

Carole H. Carpenter
Director
Ontario Folklife Centre
York University

Do you have a rhyme for us?

We hope that *Bounce Me, Tickle Me, Hug Me* will bring back memories of many loved rhymes and that some of these will be passed on to us at the Parent-Child Mother Goose Program. We especially hope to find rhymes from languages and parts of the world not represented in this book, but all rhymes are welcome. We will use them, teach them and possibly put some of them in another book.

Call or fax Sandra Carpenter-Davis
(416) 653-6475

Or contact:
Parent-Child Mother Goose Program
P.O. Box 68563
360A Bloor St. W.
Toronto, ON M5S 1X1
(416) 588-5234

x
Bounce Me, Tickle Me, Hug Me

Bulgarian

Друс, друс, конче,
От върбово клонче.
Видела го мацата,
Скочила на кацата.
Видела го мечката,
Скрила се зад печката.
Видела го лиса
И от страх се слиса.

Bouncy, bouncy, horsey
Of a willow branch;
Bounce child on your knees
Pussy cat saw it and… jumped!
Lift child in the air
Brown bear saw it and… hid!
Cover child's eyes
Red fox saw it and ran…
Run fingers up child's arm
Away!
Wave good-bye

Marta Simidchieva remembers both her babas (grannies), Lyuba Nassalevska and Nadezhda Simidchieva, doing this bouncing rhyme with her baby brother.

Caribbean (Jamaica)

Mosquito one, mosquito two,
    Twirl right first finger, then left
Mosquito jump
In a hot callaloo.
    One finger flies and tickles child's belly

        Light the lamp,
           Cover, then uncover, child's eyes with your hands
        Mosquito come,
           Twirl right first finger
        Pinch him bottom,
           Gently pinch child's bottom
        Out the lamp.
           Cover eyes again

                Mosquito one, mosquito two,
                    (Repeat actions from line 1)
                Mosquito jump
                In the ole' man shoe.
                    Pat bottom of child's foot

                        Baby canna' walk,
                        Baby canna' talk,
                        Baby canna' eat
                          Rock child from side to side
                        With a knife and fork.

Many people from Jamaica remember this rhyme in one form or another. Thanks to the women at Creating Together for sharing this version – and several others.

Caribbean (Jamaica)

This is a bouncing and clapping rhyme.

Mama buy bread,
Give baby none.

Baby get vex,
Throw himself down.

Clap hands, clap hands,
Till Mama come home.

Every mother can relate to this rhyme shared by Delver McFarlane at Creating Together.

Caribbean (St. Vincent)

Poor Henreetta
Gone to town;
She no have nothing to eat.
    Bounce child on your knees

    Poor Henreetta
    Gone to town;
    She no have nothing to eat.
        Continue bouncing

        Piece a' plantain,
            Hold up one hand and shake it
        Piece a' okra,
            Hold up other hand and shake it
        Knock upon a neighbour's door.
            Knock on child's forehead

            Piece a' plantain,
            Piece a' okra,
            Knock upon a neighbour's door.
                (Repeat actions)

Velrina Alexander, a teacher at the Parkdale Mother Goose Program, remembers her grandfather doing this rhyme/song with her in St. Vincent.

Chinese

點 虫 虫
虫 虫 飛

                            Deem chung chung
                            Chung chung
                            Fay!
                                Transliteration of spoken Cantonese

One little bug
Way over here,
   Hold up right hand, thumb and finger tips together
One little bug
Way over there,
   Hold up left hand, finger tips together
They see each other,
Fly and fly,
   Bring finger tips of both hands together

Hello!
Hello!
   Rotate hands while touching finger tips
Good-bye!
Good-bye!
   Wave good-bye with fingers
They fly away,
One here,
One there.
   Flutter fingers back to original positions

Ching Yee shares this popular Chinese rhyme with her son Alvin. Children love the fluttering hand motions ending this rhyme.

Chinese

小猴子吱吱叫，
肚子餓了不能跳，
給香蕉，還不要，
你說好笑不好笑。

*This is a bouncing rhyme.
You might also tickle the child
under the arms when you say
"Chee, chee, chee!"*

Little Monkey in a tree
Looks so hungry –
Chee, chee, chee!

Maybe he'll jump down to me?
No, he can't,
Chee, chee, chee!

Toss him a banana – wheee!
Back it comes,
Chee, chee, chee!

Little Monkey in a tree,
Are you playing games with me?

Winston and Chelsen Lee shared this and many more rhymes when they brought their two daughters, Sharon and Tina, to our West Scarborough Mother Goose Program. This rhyme is popular in Hong Kong.

French

Un poulet sur le mur
Qui picote du pain dur
Picati, picata
Lève la queue
Et puis s'en va.

Little chicken on the wall,
Hold left hand flat with palm down
Pecking at the corn and all,
Pecking here, pecking there,
*With fingers of right hand
make pecking motions on back of
left hand*
Flap your wings,
Make flapping motions with hands
Fly through the air.
"Fly" hand away

Sally Jaeger found this rhyme to use with moms and children in her baby program.
We have slightly adapted Sally's English version.

German

Das ist der Daumen,
der schüttelt die Pflaumen,
der hebt sie auf,
der bringt sie nach Haus,
und der kleine Wuzi Wuzi
ißt sie alle auf!

This one's the thumb,
Wiggle child's thumb
This one shakes the plums,
Wiggle first finger
This one picks them up,
Wiggle middle finger
This one takes them home,
Wiggle third finger
And little Wuzi Wuzi
Wiggle little finger
Eats them all up!
*Run your fingers up child's arm
and end with a tickle*

Niki Sinhart phoned her mother, Lori, in Germany
to get this rhyme to enjoy with her children, Luka and Yuri.

Greek

Πάει ο λαγός
να πιεί νερό
μέσ' στης Χαρίκλειας
το λαιμό

Here goes the rabbit,
Hoppity, hop,
To drink some water,
Sippity, sip.
> *Hop your hand up child's arm*

Where will she find it?
No, not here…
> *A little tickle under her arm*

She'll find some under
Baby's ear!
> *Tickle under child's ear*

David John James Frey has his grandmother, Harriet Xanthakos, to tell him stories and rhymes like this one. She also brought David to the Parkdale Mother Goose Program.

Hindi

नी नी बाबा नीनी
मक्खन रोटी चीनी
मक्खन रोटी हो गया
नी नी बाबा सो गया

Nee nee baba nee nee
Makkhan roti cheeni
Makkhan roti ho gaya
Nee nee baba so gaya
Transliteration

Sleep, small baby, sleep,
   Rock child gently
You've had butter
And bread
And sugar to eat.
   Put up one, then two, then three fingers
The butter,
The bread,
The sugar are gone,
   Fingers down one at a time
And my baby has gone to sleep.
   Rock gently

Micky Bhatia shared this rhyme with us at the South Asian Women's Centre. She told us this is one of the oldest rhymes from India. This rhyme sounds lovely sung to a made-up lullaby tune.

Hungarian

Csip, csip csóka,
Vak varjúcska.
Komámasszony kéreti a szekerét,
Nem adhatom oda,
Tyúkok üluek rajta.
Hess, hess, hess!

Caw, caw, jackdaw,
Blind little crow,
My old friend needs her cart
But the cart can't go.
Bounce child on your knees
The hens are sitting on it
And they say, "No!"
Stop bouncing on "No!"
But we'll chase them away –
Shoo! Shoo! Shoo!
Shoo the hens away by holding hands out flat and quickly crossing one hand over the other, repeatedly

Teacher Susan Csaszar came to Canada to work as a caregiver while learning English and finding out about our system of education. She took back many rhymes learned at the Parkdale Mother Goose Program and now teaches them to her students in Hungary.

Hungarian

Zsipp-zsúp, kenderzsúp,
Ha megázik, kidobjuk,
Zsupsz!

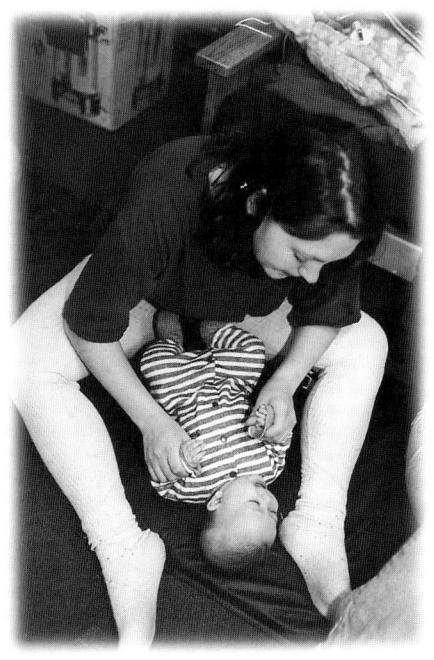

Thitch-thatch,
Hemp thatch,
If it gets wet
We throw it away –
Whoops!

You can either pick up and swing the child or rock her in your arms or on your lap. At "Whoops!" you can lower the child to the ground or drop her gently between your knees.

This is another delightful rhyme from Susan Csaszar.

Irish

Poor wee me,
When I was wee
I used to sit
On my mammy's knee.
> *Bounce child on your knees*

Her apron tore
And I fell through.
> *Open knees so child
> falls gently through*

Poor wee me,
When I was wee!
> *Hug child*

This song/rhyme was sung to Sheila Sellar by her mother, Nellie Lynch, when she was a wee lass in Ireland.

This is the way me father
Taught me how to play the fiddle:
Here and there and everywhere,
Especially in the middle!
> *Hold the child's arm outstretched
> – that's the fiddle. Use the side
> of your hand as a bow, back and
> forth. On the word "middle,"
> gently chop or tickle.*

Sheila Sellar remembers her grandfather, James Lynch, doing this rhyme with her when she was a little girl.

Italian

Bati, bati, li manini,
Adesso vene pappa,
Ti cate li ciocalatini,
E Pina li mangiera.

Clap, clap, clap your hands,
Clap child's hands
Daddy will soon be here
Bounce child on your knees
With chocolates in his pockets
Pretend to search child's pockets
To be eaten by Pina dear.
Tickle tummy

Pina Marchese remembers her mother, Domenica Marchese, saying this Calabrian rhyme to her when she was a child in Toronto.

Japanese

ふたあつ ふたあつ
なんでしょね
お目が いち に
ふたつでしょ
お耳も ほらね
ふたつでしょ

ふたあつ ふたあつ
まだあって
お手が いち に
ふたつでしょ
あんよも ほらね
ふたつでしょ

まだまだ いいもの
なんでしょね
まあるい あれよ
母さんの
おっぱい ほらね
ふたつでしょ

Two, two,
What are two?
Eyes are two – one, two.
Touch under baby's eyes
Ears are two – one, two.
Touch each ear

Two, two,
What are two?
Hands are two – one, two.
Touch each hand
Feet are two – one, two.
Touch each foot

Two, two,
What else is two?
You know, you know,
Mother's breasts are two.
Cuddle baby to you

Reiko Oki took time out from her busy job and flurry of activity around her son's wedding to share this rhyme/song.

Portuguese

Pom pom galinha, pom pom,
Ovinhos paro Mathew.
Pom pom galinha, pom pom,
Ovinhos paro Mathew comer.

Peck, peck, peck goes the little red hen;
Peck in child's palm with your first finger

Step, step, step, go her feet.
Walk fingers up child's arm

In her nest is an egg for Mathew,
Tickle under child's arm

An egg for Mathew to eat!
Touch child's mouth

At just a year old, Mathew loved to make circles in his palm when he heard this rhyme. His mother Sandy remembers her mother, Teresa Moiniz, doing it with her as a child.

Portuguese

Aqui poem a galinha o ovo e à menina (ò menino).
Papa todo vai por qui, por qui, por qui,
Chega aqui quer e que, que.

Here's the hen,
Now ain't she grand!
Tap finger on child's palm
An egg she's laid
In baby's hand.
Trace circle in child's palm
Cook it up,
Run fingers up to child's mouth
Chew it down,
Run fingers down to belly
Chickens running
Round and round.
Run fingers round and round on child's belly
Buck, buck, buck…
Peck with fingers on child's belly while making chicken noises

Fern Felix says this rhyme was passed down the generations from her two grandmothers. Aubrey Davis created the delightful English rhyme.

Punjabi (Pakistan)

چُونٹے مائیاں
کھنڈ کھیر کھایاں
نانی دا گھر آ ... آ ... آ گیا

Chuntaay my^{n}ya
Khunde kheer khay^{n}ya
Nani daa khar aaa…ghaya
Transliteration
(NB: ^{n} is nasal sound)

Ride the horsey,
> *Child faces you on lap*
> *Hold child's hands and*
> *rock forward and back*

Gee up!
> *Lift knees and stop*

And eat some sweet rice pudding.
> *Lower knees and touch*
> *child's mouth*

Ride the horsey,
Gee up!
And eat some sweet rice pudding.
> *(Repeat actions)*

See the house? See the house?
> *Shade child's eyes with your hand*

It's grandma's!
> *Point to the distance*

Zahida Ellahi in Lahore, Pakistan used to do this rhyme with her daughter, Rohelia, who now does it in Toronto with her son, Adam.

Serbian

Таши, таши, танана,
свилена је марама,
у марами шећера,
да ми дете (име) вечера.

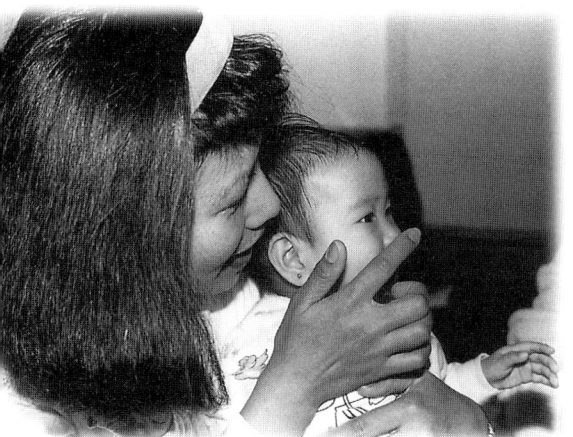

Clap, clap, clap your hands,
Clap child's hands
The scarf is made of silk;
Tickle around child's neck
And in the scarf is something sweet.
Pretend to hide something in your cupped hands
If you find it…
Open your hands slowly
It's yours to eat.
And with your hands, touch child's mouth

Tatjana Chorney heard this from both her mother, Vojna Jerkovic, and grandmother, Jusanka Jerkovic, when she was little. She now shares the rhyme with her son Nikolai and with us at the West Hill Mother Goose Program.

Spanish (Argentina)

Este chanchito fue al mercado,
Este chanchito compró un huevito,
Este chanchito lo cocinó,
Este chanchito lo peló,
Este pícaro se lo comió
Y todos lo corrieron hasta aquí.

> This little pig went to the market,
> *Wiggle child's little finger*
> This little pig bought an egg,
> *Wiggle third finger*
> This little pig cooked it,
> *Wiggle middle finger*
> This little pig peeled it,
> *Wiggle first finger*
> This little rascal ran to the house and ate it,
> *Wiggle thumb and run all your fingers up child's arm*
> And all the others went after him and… tickle, tickle, tickle!
> *And tickle under arm*

This Argentinean rhyme comes from Diana Szecket who shared it with us at the Mother Goose Program at Jessie's Centre for Teenagers. Diana also created the English version of the rhyme.

Tamil

நிலா நிலா வா வா
நில்லாமல் ஓடி வா
மலை மேலே ஏறி வா
மல்லிகைப் பூ கொண்டு வா

நடு வீட்டில் வை யே
நல்ல துதி செய் யே
வெள்ளிக் கிண்ணத்தில்
பாலும் சோறும்
அள்ளி அள்ளி ஊட்டு
குழந்தைக்குச் சிரிப்புக் காட்டு

Rock your baby gently, especially while looking at the moon

Moon, moon
Come to us, moon;
Rise over the mountains
And come to us soon.

Milk and rice in a silver dish,
Feed the baby with a silver spoon,
Play with her in the gentle
    moonlight;
Moon, moon, come to us soon.

When Soundra Siva was a young woman her mother, Vallainayaki, retaught her many rhymes so that she could share them with her children. Soundra is now a grandmother and brought wonderful rhymes to our program at the South Asian Women's Centre. In Sri Lanka, which is near the equator, the moon often rises at the time babies are fed, and so a baby may be entertained by looking at the moon and hearing this rhyme while peacefully eating.

Tamil

Each rhyme in this book has a story behind it – the story of how it came to us. This is just one such story.

A group of Tamil women had been coming to one of our programs. Some knew a lot of English, some a little, but they and their babies quietly enjoyed the rhymes we all did together. Then one day a rhyme that involved wiggling the child's fingers one at a time made the mothers laugh with pleasure. It reminded them of a rhyme from home. They began to remember it together – not all versions were the same but there was always the fun of "feeding" everyone in the family. Later, Ruth Danziger took the rhyme to a group at the South Asian Women's Centre, and it brought back memories to some of the participants who helped with the "sound" words for stirring and the creeping of the crab. Since then, people from many parts of the world have enjoyed the rhyme, sometimes changing the foods to their children's favourites, or "feeding" the people present instead of the family. Perhaps the children we play it with now will remember the rhyme with pleasure and pass it on to their children.

சோறு, பருப்பு, கிழங்கு, தயிரு, ரசம் எல்லாம் கலந்து
கீரை கடா, கீரை கடா, கீரை கடா

இது அப்பாவுக்கு, அம்மாவுக்கு, அண்ணாவுக்கு, அக்காவுக்கு
இது தம்பிக்கு, இது எனக்கு

கை கழுவி கை கழுவி காக்காவுக்கு ஊத்து
நண்டூரு நரியூரு ... நண்டூரு நரியூரு ...

We're hungry!
What will we eat?
We have some rice,
> Wiggle child's little finger

We have some dahl,
> Wiggle child's third finger

We have some potatoes,
> Wiggle child's middle finger

We have some yoghurt,
> Wiggle child's first finger

We have some soup,
> Wiggle child's thumb

So...
Stir the pot, kir-a-ka-da,
Kir-a-ka-da, kir-a-ka-da,
Kir-a-ka-da.
> Move your bent elbow round and round in the palm of your opposite hand

So...
This is for Papa,
This is for Mama,
This is for brother,
This is for sister,
And this is for you!
> Pretend to feed imaginary family from your hand

So...
The pot is empty;
Give the crumbs
To the birds.
> Brush palms together

Now...
The crab is crawling,
Nanduru, naryuru,
Nanduru, naryuru,
Keechee, keechee, keechee, keechee.
> Crawl your fingers up child's arm and end with a tickle

This rhyme was first translated for us by Mahes Parameswaran at the Gordon Ridge Mother Goose Program. We have Soundra to thank for the version written in Tamil. It is a very popular Tamil rhyme and we like to do the English version in our Mother Goose programs. Parents find it to be a useful feeding-time rhyme.

Ukrainian

Горох, бараболя, фасоля
Баба від даху летить до неба

Horoh, barabolya, fasolya
Baba veed dahoo letit do neba!
Transliteration

Peas,
> *Wiggle child's little finger*

Potatoes,
> *Wiggle child's third finger*

Beans,
> *Wiggle child's middle finger*

See grandmother
> *Wiggle child's first finger*

Fly away off the roof
To the sky!
> *While fluttering fingers,
> lift arms and fling them wide*

Pat Coles and her mother, Ann Busiak, shared these wonderful rhymes with fellow teacher Aubrey Davis, who gave them to us. Myron Dmytryshyn and Dianne Dubas also knew the rhymes and helped by writing the Ukrainian script.

Ukrainian

Аа, аа, аа, котики два,
Шарі бурі обидва.
Нічого не будуть робити
Тільки дитину бавити.

Ahh, ahh,
Two little cats,
> *Hold child's two hands or feet*

One is orange
> *Shake one*

And one is black.
> *Then the other*

The little orange cat
Chased a mouse,
"Squeak, squeak!"
> *Run fingers around on child's arm or body*

The little black cat
Rocked Petya to sleep.
> *Cuddle child and rock back and forth*

Urdu

سو جا چندا سو جا

میری راج دُلاری سو جا

(میرے راج دُلارے سو جا)

تجھے نِندیا ستارۓ سو جا

تجھے ممتا پکارے سو جا

سو جا چندا سو جا

میری راج دُلاری سو جا

Soja chanda soja
Meri raj dulari soja
(Mere raj dulare soja)
Tuje nindiya sataye soja
Tuje mamta pakare soja
Soja chanda soja
Meri raj dulari soja
Transliteration

A lullaby rhyme for rocking

Sleep, my darling moon,
Sleep…
Sleep calls to you,
So sleep…
Your mummy says,
Go to sleep.
Sleep, my baby,
Sleep…
My lovely child,
Sleep…

This rhyme was collected by Ruth Danziger at the South Asian Women's Centre where Kaneez Mian remembered it from her childhood in Pakistan. Feel free to create a tune so that you can sing it.

Vietnamese

Kià con ngựa trắng
Kià con ngựa hồng
Nhông nhông! nhông nhông!
nhông nhông!
Ngựa phi qua sông núi.

Look, there's a white horse!
Look, there's a pink horse!
*Sit child on your knees facing you,
hold her hands, shake one hand, then
the other*
Nhong nhong! nhong nhong!
Nhong nhong! nhong nhong!
Bounce child with galloping rhythm
They fly up to the mountain
And down to the sea.
Raise your knees and lower them
Nhong nhong! nhong nhong!
Nhong nhong! nhong nhong!
Bounce child again

To-Nhan Hang shared this bouncing rhyme with us at the Parkdale Mother Goose Program. To-Nhan does not remember rhymes being done with children when she was young in Vietnam, but she asked a friend who told her this rhyme.

Yiddish

Oyrele, Boyrele
Oygele, Boygele
Ekele, Bekele
Tshutshele, in mol azoy!

Earkin-Hearkin,
  Wiggle each of child's ears
Eyekin-Spykin,
  Touch beside each eye
Cheeky-Chucky,
  Gently pinch each cheek
Chin-chin-chin,
  Pat under chin
And down the hatch!
  Walk fingers up to child's mouth

Sandra Shubs (née Fischler) knows that these two rhymes from Poland have been passed down for at least four generations in her own family. She learned them from her mother, Fay Gottlieb, who learned them from her mother, Duba-Hendel Steinlauf, who learned them from her mother, Fraidel Bergman.

Yiddish

Bule, bule, butz

or

Bazoo, bazoo, butz

Bazoo, bazoo
> *Nod your head toward the child's head, twice*

Butz.
> *Bump foreheads gently together*

Bazoo, bazoo
Butz.
> *(Repeat actions)*

The goat, the goat
> *Nod your head toward the child's head, twice*

Goes bumps.
> *Bump foreheads gently together*

This playful "goat" game, also from Sandra Shubs, leaves infants and adults laughing. You can also touch your head to baby's tummy. There are many variations of this nonsense rhyme.

Inuktitut (Eastern Arctic)

This is a song a woman may sing to put her baby to sleep as she carries it on her back. We think this simple lullaby is a fitting way to end this book.

ᐊᒪᐊ, ᐊᒪᐊ
Ama, Ama

Lullaby (Humming)

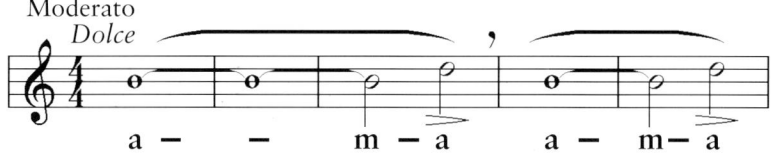

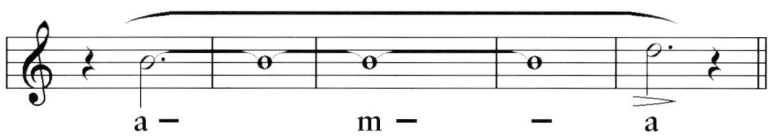

Carmen Pratt gave us this Inuktitut lullaby when she was in the Native Studies program at Trent University.

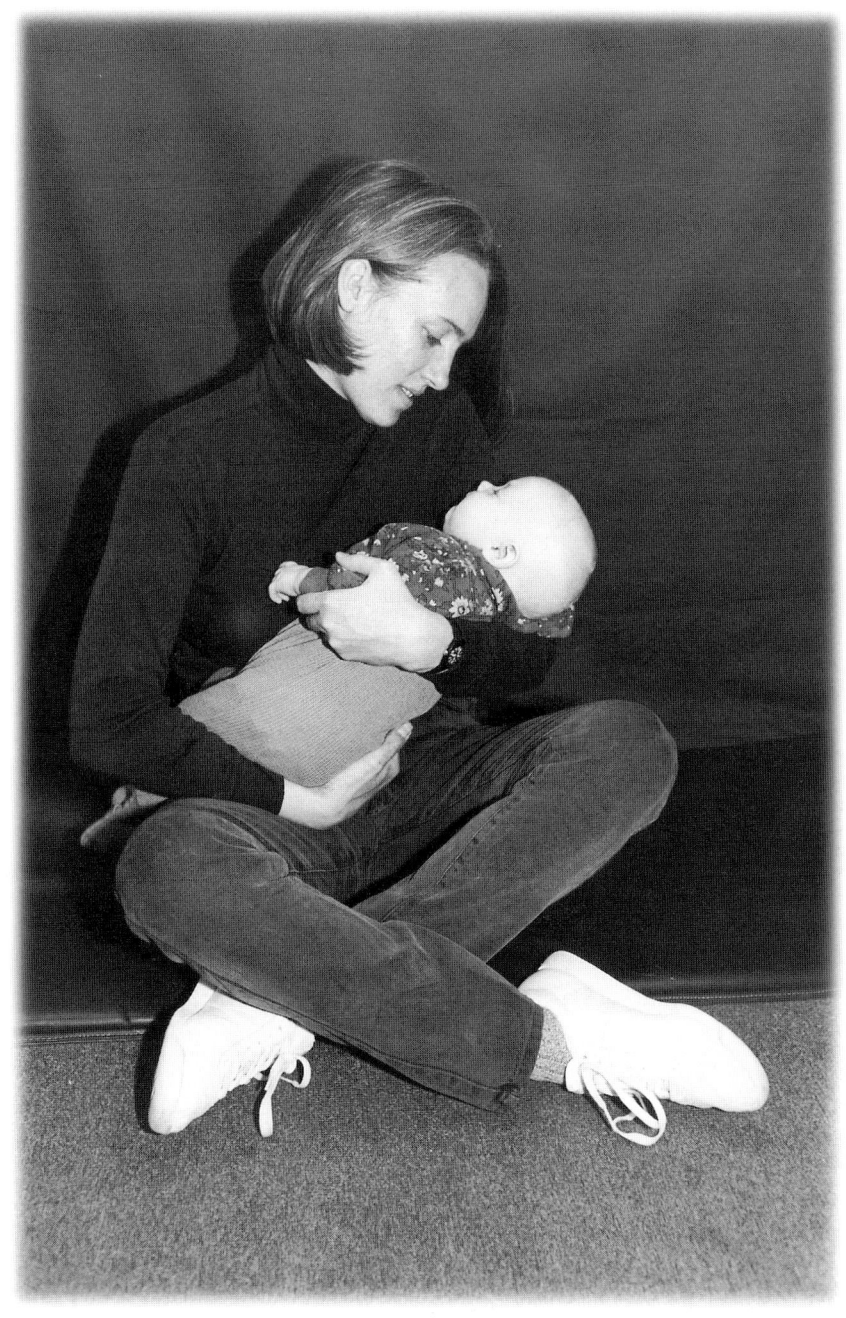

Appendices

A Note on the Text

Bounce Me, Tickle Me, Hug Me includes rhymes from many parts of the world, in twenty languages and nine alphabets. Except for the rhymes originally in English, we have given you each rhyme in both the original language and in English adaptation. In a few cases, where the rhyme is in a non-Roman alphabet and we think that readers would enjoy the sound of the original language, we have also included a transliteration that shows how the rhyme is pronounced.

Creating the English adaptations of the rhymes posed a special challenge. Rhymes used with little children are loved because of their rhythm, the sounds of the words and their interesting, sometimes nonsensical, images. These very qualities make them difficult to translate from one language to another. In *Bounce Me, Tickle Me, Hug Me* our goals were: 1) to respect the language and traditions of each rhyme; and 2) to create an English-language version of the rhyme that could be easily used and enjoyed by parents and children. These are not translations in the usual sense, but renderings which we hope convey the spirit of the originals.

The people who gave us these rhymes are bilingual and could tell us the literal meaning of the words. In some cases, this literal translation had to be only slightly changed to become a rhythmic, appealing English rhyme. Other rhymes needed to be extended or elaborated or simplified to be both meaningful and playful in English. Where our English version differs significantly from the rhyme in the original language, we have included the literal translation in an appendix so that you can compare it with our English version.

As you use this book, you will become aware that it is the outcome of many people working together. As Director of The Parent-Child Mother Goose Program, I would particularly like to thank Sandra Carpenter-Davis whose active interest in rhymes from many cultures inspired the project, Alison Dickie who worked hard in the initial stages to make it a practical reality, and Charles Casement who paid essential attention to every detail as the book came together.

The whole process of creating *Bounce Me, Tickle Me, Hug Me,* has been challenging but very rewarding. We hope you enjoy the results.

Celia Barker Lottridge
Director
The Parent-Child Mother Goose Program

Literal Translations

We offer these literal translations where they differ significantly from our English adaptations.

Bulgarian – Page 1
Bounce, bounce, horsey
Made of a willow branch.
The pussy cat saw it
And jumped on the barrel.
The bear saw it
And hid behind the stove.
The fox saw it
And was struck dumb by fear.

Chinese – Page 5
Two little bugs
See each other,
Meet,
Fly away.

Chinese – Page 6
Monkey making chee chee sound;
Hungry, could not jump.
Someone gave him banana;
He didn't want it.
Isn't that funny (strange)?

Greek – Page 9
Goes the hare
To drink water
Inside Harriet's
Neck.

Hungarian – Page 11
Cheep, cheep, jackdaw,
Blind little crow.
My old friend
Sends for her cart.
I cannot give it to her;
Hens are sitting on it.
Shoo, shoo, shoo!

Portuguese – Page 16
The chicken has eggs for Mathew.
The chicken has eggs for Mathew to eat.

Portuguese – Page 17
Here the chicken lays an egg
And the child eats it up.
It goes here, here, here.
When it gets here, pi pi pi.

Tamil – Page 21
Moon, moon,
Come, come to us.
Stay not there.
Come to us quickly,
Climbing above the mountains,
Bringing us some jasmine,
To put in the shrine room.
Let us pray for all of us.
Milk and rice in a silver dish,
Feed the baby with a silver spoon;
Make the baby laugh and play.
Moon, moon come to us.

Ukrainian – Page 25
Ah, ah, ah, two kittens are there,
Both gray and dun.
They will do nothing
But play with baby.

Here is a place to write down other rhymes that you and your family have shared and enjoyed.